I0155317

Paperlight

poems by

Claudia McGhee

Finishing Line Press
Georgetown, Kentucky

Paperlight

ACKNOWLEDGMENTS

Some of these poems first appeared, sometimes in slightly different form, in *The Nimham Times Magazine,* and *Putnam Poets Anthologies* 1990, 1991, 1992, 1994.

Many thanks to my fellow poets, Thread City Poets and Putnam Poets especially, my teachers, and, above all, my loved ones whose ongoing feedback provide me with opportunities to improve.

Publisher: Leah Maines

Editor: Christen Kincaid

Cover Art: Karl G. Jacobson

Author Photo: Karl G. Jacobson

Cover Design: Elizabeth Maines

Printed in the USA on acid-free paper.
Order online: www.finishinglinepress.com
also available on amazon.com

Author inquiries and mail orders:
Finishing Line Press
P. O. Box 1626
Georgetown, Kentucky 40324
U. S. A.

Table of Contents

Octaves..1

Twin...2

Summer Singing Walk 3

Mirrors..4

Sirocco..5

I Am Fine..6

Night Waking 7

Small Daughter 8

New 9

Occupation: Father..10

Fevers 11

Triolet...12

Aftermath 13

Preschool 14

Our Constants..15

Cold..16

Playground 17

Caesura 18

Jeans 19

Our Eclipses 20

Rented Cello...22

In Our Fifteenth Year 23

Required Meditation.......................................24

Window 25

Instincts 26

For Helen,
who believed in my poems when
just about everything else was falling apart

Sometimes your hands drift on me, milkweed's
airy silk
(*Marge Piercy, "Implications of one plus one"*)

From somewhere
a froth of seeds drifted by touched
with gold in the last light
of a lost day, going with
the wind as they always did.
(*Philip Levine, "Milkweed"*)

Octaves

Before you kiss me, nurture octaves:
Harbor thunder in your bones and mist in your breath.
When you reach for me, offer one heart stopping moment,
that instant *before* your hands grasp my wrists and I am safe.

Devote your lips to me the way the lightless
subterranean river nuzzles the etched cavern wall.
Move the absolute length of your body against me,
leave no room for echoes and barely enough for air.

Mind the heated mantra of my heartbeat, and if you release me,
stay close. Listen for the gentle breeze within our stillness,
lure me back with the consecrated hymn of your need—
teach me this holy braille of your love.

Twin
for Helen, 8/23/1951–10/29/2006

In you, in me, hunger and passion
are twin sisters, are the surprise
of dangerous ideas in well used
lively bodies. Sensing your heartbeat,
I name you; when you sing,
you cradle me—our common breath
spins fragrance across our fingers.
What we see, we share, and in sharing
we fly, we careen through curves on two
wheels then tumble into tears.
We gorge on words, ghosts, hope, and dust,
and fill all those soul places left empty
by our men. When we touch,
we wonder if this is the way
to grow wise.

Summer Singing Walk

That summer I walked,
determination dragging fatigue uphill
like a lame leg.

I walked the pavement's scorched
pebbled skin and you rode,
the gentle waves rocking you
suspended there
in the basket of my belly.

That summer I sang,
struggling to weave melodies past
the stinging, breath-stopping dust in my throat.

I sang and you stopped paddling your elbows
knees and toes inside me.
You lay quiet in the vanishing wash
of vibrations, hearing me
with every cell in your unfinished body.

That summer, together we were ready
when the tides turned and wave after wave
swelled around you above you behind you
inside me, nosing you centimeter
by centimeter out of my sea.

Mirrors

Upper East Side streetlights, headlights,
even the dazzling ricochets
of store window displays splinter
my evening dark. Echoes divide,

follow me up four hollow flights
to the gathering where he waits.
In this place, in front of others,
he does not free his hands to sculpt

his answering against my skin.
The calm way he watches me is
brighter than shrill sun on flagrant
orange leaves. The dense pelt of his

gaze is incomprehensible.
I know him as I know the closed
and white door of a stranger's home
glimpsed from the highway; know only

his face, eyes and arcing lips—know
it is his silence I will bed.

Sirocco

I sting swift, hot, over the slow rockslide
of you; rasp, scour and whip with dirt stripping
words your heavy jutting thrust. On quick wing
I sear the exposed rim of your face, glide
high in rising thermals, plunge fast inside
your vast surprise of earth. I rush, seeking
relief in your quiescent stone; slipping
along fault lines, our dry and moist collide.

You catch my storm, cup my wild, agile flight,
and settle your steady weight into me.
Tremors travel your veins, shift to bedrock,
focus my urgent freedoms to one point.
Within this quieting courtship, your need
contains me with the reticence of rock.

I Am Fine

This is spring and somehow, I am fine.
These dandelion greens, so sweet
before flowering, jagged amid new grass.

Before chicks arrive, yellow feathered wings
dip and swoop, beaks snapping
on poplar fluff, seeds, shredded bark.

This year's torrent of wind and rain cracks
last year's milkweed pods
from stems, paperlight, empty, drowning.

This shower of petals, serviceberry white,
adheres, smears,
withers on my windshield.

I am fine and this is spring. Somehow
I am fine
until you touch me.

Night Waking

I lie awake, night caught in your slow sighs.
Trapped only by the pulsing sleep you weave,
I touch the heart of each breath as it dies

and mourn, even as your body denies
that lapse, that ending, and again you breathe.
I lie awake, night caught in your slow sighs,

in the stillness of your hands hips and thighs.
The quiet pause of you does not deceive;
I touch the heart of each breath as it dies,

feel the harsh bite of loss in stunned surprise:
time with you, like breath, does pass, does recede.
I lie awake, night caught in your slow sighs,

hear lissome songs released—low lullabies
airy and open, whisper brief reprieve.
I touch the heart of each breath as it dies

and in its deep red beat, I recognize
you. In the grotto of your sleep, I grieve.
I lie awake, night caught in your slow sighs—
I touch the heart of each breath as it dies.

Small Daughter

Empath, chameleon child,
at ten months, enthralled,
you watch my face, my mouth
savoring my favorite apple.

With my offer to try some,
you reach up, release
your doubt, surrender
your preference, and devour
my pleasure so completely
that even the shadows on your face
mirror mine.

I am relieved
when you release me
by refusing
another piece.

New

I ride the long wet rush of you.
The slow streamings of your finger
trace lips and breasts, tease limbs alive; new
sweetnesses surge, recede, and linger.

The slow streamings of your finger
caress me with intimate, flickering fire.
Sweetnesses surge, recede, and linger,
return with the force of seizing desire

caress me with intimate, flickering fire.
Beneath me, your hips and back lift, incite—
return with the force of seizing desire.
Caught in your flaring, I ignite;

beneath me, your hips and back lift, incite.
You thrust deep, beyond habit, then quicken;
caught in your flaring, I ignite.
The tense coil of my womb springs open,

you thrust deep, beyond habit, then quicken.
This time our union, our climax is new:
the tensed coil of my womb springs open,
I ride the long, wet rush, of you.

Occupation: Father

I can almost hear
the silent impulse of her need
leap—before it tugs her to her feet
in the room upstairs
and partners her search
through our house.
I can almost see
her breath as it swings the treble
questioning touch of her voice
into and out of each cluttered room.
A door slams; her feet pause,
there is quiet at the top of the stairs.
Her hand begins sliding, squeaks
on the high gloss handrail,
her small heels hit
solid and sharp on hollow
pine stairs, mark her progress
through the kitchen, the den—
until she streaks into the study
and squirms up onto my lap.
She wriggles against me,
her hugs punctuated with hushed
sighs of "Daddy!"
I set aside the newspaper with its illuminated
faces of dry-boned children, debilitated mothers,
and enfold her in my arms.
As I press my face to her hair,
I feel the newsprint smear on my fingers
and wonder: but what about
the fathers?

Fevers

It is 2AM when I touch you again,
the fever thrown from your small forehead
presses against my hand.

In the dim clown-held light,
I pause beside you to breathe hot sheets,
shadows, the taste of mucus
choking your chest.

Later, glowing in my own bed,
your heat dances inside me the way the word
"daughter" hisses and licks through my life,
waking me when I most need to sleep.

Triolet

The way you breathe
wreathes my name in sighs.
Nearing release,
the way we breathe
avowals seethe,
need tells no lies.
The way you breathe
wreathes my name in sighs.

Aftermath

With scarred fingers
I poke through the shattered
debris of our latest fight,
muttering (as always),
"there's a lesson here—
somewhere."

I pick up pieces, firm
sliding curves ending
in deadly blades.
Gingerly I set them down.

This mess on the floor—
impossible
to put together again,
even the dust is dangerous.

Two days later,
we stumble against each other
in the crowded confines of the kitchen
and the physical shock of your body
stops me.

Preschool

This season all her stick figures
have one ear (the left one),
just one wide eye—
only the left side
of every red smile.
She scribbles thick
promising hair
on half circle heads,
and five fingers
balloon
from single, crooked arms.
She works from crown
to toe: straight
crayon purple stripes
of torso,
left legs (in orange)—
each left shoe
brown, and poised
in air.

Our Constants

Couplings
sparked by our keen fingers' greeting
between
bed sheets. Honey and ice meeting
words. Our
hive of garnered memories slides
beyond
sipped moments, burnt lips healing; glides
along
the flume and striding span of years.
Newborn
and torn promises fly through fears,
embed
in eyes, hips. Our fugue recurves, thrums,
returns:
Instant after instant becomes
body.

Cold

I can almost ignore the season,
the lash of this angry storm.
Within the warm nesting of our home,
I can almost forget
this cold coiling heavy
outside under the eaves,
this rushing across our sturdy
pillared porch, and winter
slicing iced gutters
gorged, solid, sagging.

Beneath roof peaks drifting with snow,
between flannel sheets,
we flourish in the thin moisture
of midnight;
breathing and alive, our loving
coats the windows
crystalline, sure.

We stack firewood and blankets,
stoke stove and bed,
invoke our thin shell of safety
for the night, until daylight

I step outside, alone,
dive into driving blasts;
the glacial whip chips
electric and vicious at my bones.
I stumble inside to you
cracked and keening, bearing
this blizzard's cold in my hands,
my bleak biting gift
as I beg you to kiss my lips,

my face made of wind.

Playground

You careen around this dusty playground,
the sturdy intent of your small body propelling you
from one metal and wood structure
to another. I follow you, mother-linked
to your calls of mastery
your demands for help.
With scraped hands and dirty feet you push
across flattened grass to scale tall ladders
and puddle through mud to slide down poles.
Again and again your skin squeaks against metal
on the corkscrew slide.
Over under and through the barrels, climbing reaching
dropping crawling, inside outside and down the ramps—
the sandbox, the seesaw, the monkey bars
     the points of weightlessness
     at either end of a swing
     swinging
     higher, higher.
In your body's concentration, I am only
a steadying circle around your waist
a boost up
a soft touch on your cheek after a fall.

Caesura

In the wood-edged kitchen
amidst the rush and clatter of holiday meal making,
your arms open a space for me,
carve a long slow moment out of time.
Inside this circle I close my eyes,
press my cheek against your chest.

The sigh of coffee on your breath
drifts around me, eases me
from the realm of steamy, lid lifting potatoes.
Your firm fingers massage the cords along my spine,
banish the smells of hot pot metal,
browning biscuits, gravy.

Your warming hands travel down my back,
weave across the low hungry hollows of my hips.
Like the sharp tang of cranberry-orange chutney,
heat jolts through me as your arms tighten,
urge me to quicken the upward surging of your blood,
draw me against the heavy swelling under your clothes.

Jeans

Leaning into a steamy
sweet smelling cloud,
I pull your well worn jeans
out of the dryer, one hot pair
after the other.

Groping in the cavern
for the last damp waistband
and set of white frayed cuffs,
I wince at the sudden bite
of a hot rivet on my hand.

I snap irregular creases
from supple legs,
gently stretch straight
the twisted bias
from thigh to calf.

With hands that drink
the fast fading warmth,
I smooth the stiff zipper flap
and flatten the faded blisters
of bulging knees.

I fold and make tall
unsteady piles
of your soft sturdy pants,
then tuck them tightly
in your dresser drawer.

Our Eclipses

These evenings begin early, your bare skin
a lesson against mine, a joy. Your palm
opens in our bed, flowering with sleep
against my thigh, spreads something vast, burning,
fastens the strands of my life in your web.
Together we discover our raking

needs, watch our daughter's keen intent raking
humus, rock. She finds a flattened snakeskin,
asks does the tarantula spin a web?
She plays monkey, begs coconuts, climbs palm
trees, pokes at grey coals in the grill: burning
fingers sting forever. She whimpers; sleep

slips in, escapes, 'til she finds us asleep
and naps. The next hushed day I spend raking
leaves into crisp drifts, drink the strong burning
wind and sky. The rake handle worries skin
hidden under gloves into blisters, palm
raw, etched, inescapable as the web

love has woven through her room. Spider web
baths, stories, birthdays catch us the way sleep
catches her breath, soothes her. She hugs the palm-
sized plush unicorn—silver horn raking
the dark keeps her safe. I brush her pale skin,
my fingertip gifts unspoken, burning.

You and I coax twigs, coals into burning,
feed the woodstove stout logs, shake loose its web
of heat in the room where we bare our skin
again; and learn, again, the bite of sleep
lost to harsh voices, words clawing, raking
quick demands. It's as though I press my palm

in smashed glass, then with my blood, trace your palm.
My snarled yearnings arc our bed, burning
ribbons trail, aching betrayals raking
days before subsiding. I spin a web
of questions you will never hear. In sleep
we meet, break day to kiss, touch skin-to-skin,

balance palm-to-palm. We three weave this web—
rescue burning days, lost nights; drift from sleep
on the raking rocking touch of bare skin.

Rented Cello

The day before, she told us
it couldn't be brought home
on the school bus, but, yes,
it *would* fit in our car.
She warned that it was beat up
and screechy scratchy,
and when she held the bow
like the teacher said, the frog
pinched her thumb.
She showed us how
with a chopstick.
She showed me how heavy
with two long flat scraps of wood—
but not so wide, not so
wide. She perched on the chair,
knees apart, elbow crooked,
her hand before her chest
with the chopstick. Her other hand
flew up beside her head, and floated,
askew, and she sighed she was
lucky: it was just
the right size and the case
had a zipper right down the front—
only, each time, she needed someone
to hold it open.

In Our Fifteenth Year

The first time,
you blamed fatigue.

After the second time,
even when I pressed my cheek
against your damp belly
and took you in my mouth,
you lay still.

The third time, only silence, only
the slow opening of your fingers
when you slept. I stayed awake,
questions the texture and taste of salt
dissolving inside me.

Required Meditation

I breathe the metallic redolence
of her three thousand mile trip,
suck the essence of her Away
into my blood like oxygen.

I roll this disjunction
between mother and young child
in my mouth, notice my sudden pain
like saliva starting at the whip of jalapeno.

I close my eyes press my cooling skin
to this queer unfocused emptiness,
and discover the thin film of its moisture
spreading over me like dew.

Window

When our life together becomes a city
and the entanglements of everyday
thicken into a slum of gesture, invective and habit,
I follow the iridescent reds of taillights
vanishing in gasoline spills of color,
rummage through intersections and alleys after clues,
then return to our bed by the window.

When I inhale your scent in this place I know best,
the cool breeze of your hand on my breast
flings a scant path out the open window—
you slip away along its promise and I rise in pursuit
like a twist of paper airborne between buildings,
lifting past other open windows, above chimneys and spires—
and I find you again, unfurling against the clear night sky.

Instincts

Two redwing blackbirds rise among the pale
narcissus; blue jays tip the petal veil.
Your dreams were our life, filled day and night sky;
fledglings and hunger the reasons to fly.
Red-tailed hawk lifts wing, clasps vole bloody, frail.

Your visions were thirsty, every detail
goldfinch vivid, drumming ruffed grouse loud. Quail
scratches after bugs, seeds; kicks leaves awry.
        Two redwing blackbirds rise.

Rapacious goshawk dives, grasps only tail
feathers. Crows' retreat: complete countervail!
Wrens flick in wallows, dusty, ashen, dry.
I know now how my desire died, why
I left you then. This was the fairy tale:
        Two redwing blackbirds rise.

Claudia McGhee has been a writer since 8th grade, experimenting with every genre, and has spent much of her adult writing life working on poetry. She is currently an active member of the Thread City Poets, Willimantic, CT, and has recently read at the Springfield City Library's "Literary Arts Spotlight" program.

Claudia has studied poetry and fiction writing with Jerome Badanes, Billy Collins, Carolyn Forché, Dana Gioia, Jewelle Gomez, Marie Howe, Kate Knapp Johnson, Galway Kinnell, Thomas Lux, Dr. Marc Straus, and Paul Violi.

Claudia's poems have appeared in *Aileron, Asylum Annual, Connecticut River Review, Dutchess Anthology, Fresh Ink, Impetus, Let the Poets Speak, Lunch, The Nimham Times Magazine, Primal Voices, Putnam Poets anthologies, Slipstream, White Plains H.O.G. News, White Pond Reflections,* and *Zephyr.*

By day, Claudia is a software technical writer who designs, implements, writes and delivers single-source topic libraries for enterprise systems, and contributes to every activity relevant to explaining those systems. She has worked as an employee and consultant for large and small companies, including IBM Corporation, SunGard iWORKS P&C (US) Inc. (aka Insurance Software and Systems, Inc.), 1-800FLOWERS.COM, Donald Grenier Corporation, Centric Consulting LLC, Adecco Engineering & Technology, and Hallmark Total Tech Inc. She is currently employed by Optum Inc. in Hartford, CT as an information designer and technical writer.

Claudia grew up on Long Island and graduated from SUNY Geneseo. Before moving to Connecticut, Claudia was the Poet in Residence and Executive Administrator of the Putnam Poets at the Putnam Arts Council in Mahopac, NY for four years. As Executive Administrator, she managed the group's various activities, including: facilitating the bi-monthly peer workshops, making arrangements for mentored workshops, setting up audience-participation poetry readings in libraries and local parks, and inviting guest poets to read. She handled all of the group's public relations needs and wrote the grants required to obtain necessary funding.

While living in Mahopac, Claudia wrote the weekly "Writers' Spotlight" column for the *Putnam Courier-Trader Newspaper*, contributed material to Guide Communications' Getting-To-Know publications, and was a volunteer grant writer for local organizations.

In addition to being a mother, mate, and employee, Claudia has edited Dr. Edmond Chibeau's *Performance Scripts: Prime Numbers* published by Red Dust, Inc. New York. She has also provided copy editing and eBook conversion services for Larry E. Zimmerman's series of Amston Lake books.

www.ingramcontent.com/pod-product-compliance
Lightning Source LLC
LaVergne TN
LVHW041328080426
835513LV00008B/637